Uncle Harry

'Mary don't hear us!' [by Uncle Harry].

Uncle Harry

'Mary don't hear us!' [by Uncle Harry].

ISBN/EAN: 9783742857996

Manufactured in Europe, USA, Canada, Australia, Japa

Cover: Foto ©ninafisch / pixelio.de

Manufactured and distributed by brebook publishing software
(www.brebook.com)

Uncle Harry

'Mary don't hear us!' [by Uncle Harry].

TIM THE NEWSBOY.

CONTENTS

CHAPTER I.

CHAPTER V.

CHAPTER VI.

CHAPTER I.

TIM THE NEWSBOY.

BECAUSE our hearts have become steeled, and our ears deaf to the song of the "frozen-out gardeners," and of the "one-armed mariners," and others of whom such impostors are a type, are we therefore to close our eyes to the varied kinds and degrees of misery with which our great cities abound? By no means.

The child in trouble—a little one crying in the streets, unbefriended and alone—a manly boy, struggling against unkindness, hoping even against hope, are objects of pity, and subjects for the exercise of our most active benevolence. Where is the individual so callous that he can hear, without one motion of pity, the sobbings of a child in distress? Can one be found so utterly insensible to the cry of suffering as to pass by on the other side rather than make a single effort for its relief, or for the comfort of the swelling, bursting heart?   Should such an individual exist, I have no desire for his company.   On the contrary, I would fain have a heart weighed down by the sorrows of others, and fired with an earnest longing to assist the really deserving.   It is this feeling which induces me to note the cries and watch the countenances of those whom I find in our public thoroughfares plying their daily occupation.

The newsboy — who notices him?   Many a man; but who pities him, practically?   Only one here and there.   Yet he may need our pity and our help.   A boy of about twelve years went singing his papers along the street.   The day was cold, the wind was piercing, and accompanied by a driving rain.   The child's face was blue, his hands were red, while the water found its way into his shoes.   His clothes—they were but an apology for a covering to a poor shivering frame.   I pitied him—yes, I pitied him, as I heard him cry in tremulous tones, "*Telegraph, sir! Telegraph!*"

As I walked along, he ran by my side, and looking eagerly into my face, continued his appeal, "*Telegraph*, sir! *Telegraph!*" I had already supplied myself with a copy from a lad whom I had previously met. Still I was interested in the boy, and turned to see how others were affected. Sometimes the crowd ceased in its pulsations for a moment, and eager-visaged men caught at the paper, put the penny into the boy's hand, and hurried onwards. And then the newsboy would hitch up his trousers, pull on more firmly the queer old cap that hugged his crown, and break out afresh with the dismal sing-song peculiar to his vocation.

Many, alas!—at least, so I thought—treated him as a mere machine, a body without a soul, without feeling or affection, a something utterly different in constitution from themselves. His attire was mean and scanty, it is true, and the melancholy sing-song in which he indulged was decidedly unattractive; hence it was, perhaps, that the proud and thoughtless deigned not to notice him. They forgot, or had never read or seen, that moss grows upon gravestones, that

the ivy clings to the mouldering pile, and that
mistletoe springs from the withering branch ;
and that something green, something fair to
the sight, and even grateful to the heart, will
yet twine around, and grow out of the seams
and cracks of the most desolate temple of the
human soul.

As I watched the movements of the newsboy
these facts were deeply impressed upon my mind.
The expression of his countenance was remark-
ably pleasant, and my heart was drawn toward
him as I observed his bright black eye, indicat-
ing unusual intelligence, peeping out, like a ray
of sunshine, from behind a cloud. The time of
day, however, called my attention to other
matters, and I was compelled to hasten to my
place of business.

The next day the weather was finer, and the
cold had sensibly decreased. I set out early, with
the determination of seizing an opportunity of
conversing a little with the lad, and if possible
getting at his history. The morning had consi-
derably advanced, however, before I was able to
carry out my intention.

"Do you go to Sunday school, my boy?" I inquired, as soon as the crowd was sufficiently thinned for me to get near enough to speak to him.

"No, sir; I haven't got any clothes but these that I've got on, and I'm not fit to go to school, nor church, nor anywhere else."

I endeavoured to convince him that his clothes would not be a hindrance if he were only willing to go, but in vain; he adhered to the expression that he was "not fit to go anywhere."

"I am very sorry to hear that," I observed; "it is a sad thing to live without instruction either on Sunday or week-day. I must see whether I cannot find a kind friend who can give you something to wear, that you may make a tidy appearance on the Lord's day."

"If you do, it won't be any good, sir; father takes everything he can get hold of, and I can't keep tidy anyhow."

"That is sad news; but have you no friends?"

"No; I haven't got one that is worth *that*," snapping his fingers.

"I can tell you of a Friend," said I, "who should be more than all the world to you; and He is willing to be *your* friend."

"What's his name, plase, sir?"

"His name is Jesus. Do you know anything about Him?"

"I've heard the name; but I don't know Him, and I'm sartin sure I never saw Him."

"If you don't know anything about Him, the sooner you go to Sunday school the better; for there you will be told a great deal about Him. They won't mind your clothes being torn."

The only reply, however, that I could obtain was the one repeated already, "I am not fit to go anywhere." This therefore seemed to be an appropriate time for asking him another question.

"Where do you expect to go to when you die?" was my inquiry.

"To hiven, sir," was his confident reply.

"But you are not fit to go there," said I, "if you don't know anything about Jesus. We can only get to heaven through Him."

"I don't know anything about Him," said he; "but me mother says I shall go to heaven, for I

haven't done nobody any harm; and she asks
Mary—the blessed Virgin—every night to make
it all right for us. She says if I'm a good boy,
and sells my papers, and says my prayers to
the blessed mother of God, I'm sure to go to
hiven, as sartin sure as if I was there already."

"But don't you know," I asked, "that there is
another place where people go to when they die?
Those who don't love Jesus go there. Do you
know what place it is?"

"Yes—but I can't think of the name."

"I mean hell."

"No, that isn't it," said he, "it's a quarer sort
o' name nor that;" and looking down a moment
the word came to his mind—"it's pruggerty I
means; that's the place."

"Purgatory," I observed.

"Oh no, sir, not that; it's pruggerty's the
name: me mother says it is."

"And, pray, what kind of a place is that?"

"Why, as soon as people dies and gets to the
door of heaven, me mother says an angel weighs
'em, and them as weighs heavy are pitched
right over into pruggerty, and them as is light

goes up in the scale, and are taken right into hiven."

"What makes the people heavy?" I inquired, for I wanted to teach him an important truth in as few words as possible.

"Me mother says it's sins as make 'em heavy."

"What sins?"

"Lying and swearing and stealing, and the like o' them things."

"*You* are a sinner, and yet you tell me you expect to go to heaven when you die."

"I don't lie and swear and steal, and them's the sins that make 'em heavy."

"Still you are a sinner in the sight of God."

"I don't know about that," he replied; "but me mother says the praste has never said a word about our going to pruggerty. He knows we haven't got anything to pay to clear us; and we don't lie and steal, and so we are sure to go to hiven."

"Not so sure," said I; "but come, the time is gone, and I have missed one train—another day I will try and have some more talk with you."

How sad, thought I, that so shrewd a boy should know so little of his duty and destiny, and that he should believe a lie! and I longed for another opportunity of telling him more about Jesus.

CHAPTER II.

HAVING an hour to spare on the following afternoon, I made my way to the spot where I had
met with the newsboy on the previous day,
hoping that I should again find him in that fre-
quented locality. But I was disappointed. He
had gone. I wandered on, turning first into a
narrow street hard by, and thence into an open
space, intending to return in a few moments, as
by that time he might again have arrived at his
favourite haunt. I had not gone far before I observed, in an open space, a group of persons
gathered around a tall, energetic individual, who
occupied a temporary stand, and appeared to be
addressing the crowd. As my eye scanned the
assemblage, I discovered the newsboy. His

bundle of papers had lessened to one or two copies only, and he was eagerly devouring the words of the orator. I stood near and looked on. The lecturer evidently felt quite at home, and knew well how to suit his language to the audience before him. His appeal was decidedly stirring, and adapted to the object in view. A slight Scottish accent lent beauty to his eloquence. One sentence struck the ear of the attentive newsboy, it was this,—"His father was a drunkard, puir, puir child—there's naething at home for him, not even a crust in the auld closet. He must work the day long, tramping through summer's heat and winter's storm. He must hear the curses of his father, and witness the tears of his mother. He has no warm clothes, and his little heart swells nigh to bursting when he passes the well-dressed children of sober parents. And who pities him?" he asked, raising his eyes towards heaven. "Does the rum-seller? Nae—he hides his eyes from his tears. Does the rich man? Nae—too often he frowns him from his doorstep, and from the sweet smell of the kitchen where the meat is roasting.

Do the angels pity him? Yes—for what else but the wings of the angels could keep the puir boy warm? Doesn't God pity him? Oh, dinna ask that question, for God is specially the God of the drunkard's bairn."

Poor boy! The papers hung upon his arm, but his attention was absorbed. Salt tears filled his eyes, and coursed quickly down his cheeks; his lips quivered, and sobs welled up from his throat. "Alas! alas!" thought I, as the dismal truth flashed across my mind, "and he is a drunkard's child." I was about to speak to him, but he was off. Quickly had he brushed away the tears with his ragged sleeve, and with a choking voice had again taken up the burden of his song—"*Telegraph! Telegraph!*" But the words fell slowly from his lips; nevertheless, there was heart in them.

Yet it seemed as though he could not leave the spot. Once more he returned and listened—I overheard him say, "Oh, misther, misther, say something for me father." In his young face there was a strange mixture of entreaty, joy, hope, and misery, the influence of which, one would imagine,

THE STREET LECTURER.

even the strongest will would have found it diffi-
cult to resist. "Oh, misther," said the small voice
again, "tache me father not to be a drunkard."

The voice, although it did not reach the ear of
the lecturer, went to my heart. "Where is your
father?" I inquired. He pointed out a man
clothed in rags, leaning against a gas lamp. Poor
fellow! his bloodshot eyes! I noticed with pain
his haggard countenance; he *was* a pitiable
object. Presently he staggered away, and his
child, the little newsboy, with tears unshed and
sobs unspoken, went about his business, crying
once more in tremulous tones, "*Telegraph*, sir!
Telegraph!"

I followed him, and placing my hand upon his
shoulder, observed, "And so that was your father?"

"Yes, sir," he replied, with a deep-drawn sigh.

"Well, well," said I, endeavouring to comfort
him, "let us hope that he will some day become
a sober man."

"I wish he would, sir; for he bates me, and
scolds me, and takes all that I get by me papers
whenever he can, and spends it."

"That is very sad indeed," said I, "and very

unkind; but still we will hope for the best. My
little fellow," I added, in as gentle a tone as I
could command, "where is your home?"

"In Bear Alley," he replied; "but you won't
come to *our* house, will ye, sir?"

"Why should I not?" I asked.

"It's such a quare place, sir—it won't suit ginnelmen. The like o' you never comes to ours.
Father's not often there at all; and when he is,
he is not fit to be seen, nor mother neither. I
don't mean but what she's as clane as she can be,
but then she hasn't got any clothes to see
ginnelmen in."

True, the house was quite out of my way, and
in a part of the city which, so far as my feelings
were concerned, I did not care to visit. Following
my leader, however, I walked briskly onward
until I reached the place which the little newsboy called home. We went up a narrow alley,
then up a flight of well-worn steps, which led
into a wooden building that looked as if it were
on the eve of dissolution. I confess that at first
I felt almost afraid to follow, lest I should fall
into a den of thieves, or into even worse com-

pany. But as I was on an errand of mercy, and
felt sure that the Lord would take care of me,
I went on, and up two pair of stairs more, following my little conductor until I reached the room
in which he spent his nights. His home, to be
sure ; but what a home ! A pale-looking, thin
woman was seated on a stool near some ashes in
the fireplace. No signs of comfort. A heap of
straw in the corner, with some rags, appeared to
be the only bed they possessed.

The mother received her boy with a saddened
smile. "Why, Tim," said she, "an' sure you ain't
brought a ginnelman to such a place as this ?"

"Well, mother, he wanted to come."

"A wretched place for ye to come to, yer
honour," she said.

"A visit to your home," said I, "may do us
both good."

She looked doubtingly.

"Where is your husband ?" I asked.

"I don't know, yer honour," she replied, with
a sigh. "He goes out of a morning, and we niver
see him agin afore it's morning agin. He has
a bad way."

"Does he drink, then?" I suggested.

"It isn't as I likes to say a word agin him, poor sowl; but he does."

A moment's pause; and in that brief moment many thoughts rushed into my mind. A drunkard's home, thought I, and yet home. Here is a mother who loves her son, and a son who loves his mother; and it is a mother's love makes even this wretched place home to the boy.

"Tim," said the woman, somewhat abruptly, "go on and see if ye can borrow a penny loaf at Mike's; tell 'em I'll pay as soon as I've done the scrubbing at the lady's to-morrow."

"Don't borrow it," I said; "here, boy, is a sixpence; go to the baker's and buy a loaf."

Away he went. As soon as he was out of the room, "Yer honour," said she, "you said that it'd do ye good to come here. I can't see what good ye'll get here."

"I shall get good in this way," I replied: "if I go home with a more thankful heart than I have had for a long time, and am hence-forth more grateful to God for the comforts that I enjoy, then I shall have gained good by coming."

"Ye're right, no doubt. I ain't got any comforts."

"None at all?" said I.

"Why, yes, I forgot myself. That boy o' mine is a comfort to me; the only comfort I have. Poor boy! he tries hard to get a crust for his poor mother. But as for his father,"—and she wiped the tears from her eyes.

"I know all about it," said I, "your boy has told me. Your husband is not kind to either of you; but let us hope better things."

"So I says sometimes, and I asks the blessed Virgin; and no doubt she'll get her Son to tache O'Leary his duty to his poor wife and child."

"You seem to think that the Virgin Mary can help you?"

"Oh, yes and sartin sure I am she can."

"I fear," said I, seriously, "you are sadly mistaken. Mary has no power at all. You must ask God, for Jesus Christ's sake, to help you."

"But I don't know anything about that way

o' asking for anything I want. I allays do what the praste tells us."

"And what is that?"

"Why, he tells us to ask the blessed Virgin to talk to her Son about it."

"But the Bible does not teach us so," said I. "That book tells us of only one way, and that is through Jesus Christ. It tells us that there is 'only one Mediator between God and men, the man Christ Jesus,' and that there is 'none other name under heaven given among men whereby we must be saved,' but the name of Jesus."

"Well, I never heard that afore," said the poor woman; "the praste always towld me that I must ask Mary.—Och! there now, yer honour, ye tache me to say Mary—the blessed Virgin forgive me! Well, I was sayin' the praste said I was to ask the blessed Virgin, and that I niver should get an answer if I didn't."

"Have you no Bible?" I inquired.

"No, yer honour; our praste says it ain't right for us ignorant people to read that Book, bekase we can't understand it; it's only for wise, larned folk. Besides, he says *he* can tell us all we want to know."

"But," said I, "He whose word should be a lamp to our feet, and a light unto our path, tells us a very different thing; he commands us to 'search the Scriptures,' and to walk in the truth and make His word the rule of our life: for we shall be all judged by it at last."

Here I was interrupted by Tim's return; and as I wished that they should enjoy their frugal meal together and alone, I left them, promising to call on them again soon.

CHAPTER III.

"LET US ASK JESUS RIGHT STRAIGHT."

"OH, mither, mither!" said Tim, as he entered the room almost breathless, "I've seen such a sight. What d'ye think?"

"Don't know, child; but it seems to have made ye run."

"No, that didn't make me run; but ye know I niver stay about, but get home as soon as I can when I've sold me papers."

"Right, child, and ye're a downright darling, that ye are. Come, tell us all about it."

"Well, mother, I saw a man with a little coffin in his arms, and he put it on a stone wall, and stopped to rest a bit. He looked so bad."

"Depind upon it," said his mother, "he knew the child the coffin was for."

"Yes, mother, I'm sure he did. I heard him telling a little girl that asked him, all about it."

" What did he say, then ?"

" Why, he said, ' God bless you, child—ye're a little angel. God has sent ye to me. May the spirit of her I love 'tend and shield ye.' I heard him say that."

"And did he tell the little girl who the coffin was for ?"

" Yes, mother ; he said it was for his niece, and then began to cry. And the little girl told him to cheer up, because he will meet her again when he dies, if he'll only be good ; and, oh, she talked so nicely ! I heard her say this; I am sartin sure she did, every word of it. She said, ' Me mother says we shall meet *my* little sister in hiven, if we love God, and hate sin, and tell the truth, and do to others as we'd have thim do to us.' And then she looked so sorry, and the tears ran down her face ; but she soon wiped thim away with her pocket handkerchief, and said to the man, ' You'll try to meet the little girl in hiven, won't you ?' "

" What did the man say to that ?" asked his mother. " *I* shouldn't have been able to speak."

her as if he hardly knew what to think of her, and he asked her to pray for him."

"The blessed Virgin save her!" said Mrs. O'Leary. "Mayhap she said she'd ask her."

"No, mother, she didn't; but she said she would pray to God for him every night before she went to bed, and if he'd go to church on Sunday he'd hear the minister pray for him, because he always prays for people in throuble. And then she put a little book into his hand, and she bid him good-bye and ran off as fast as she could. As she passed me she put this into my hand, and towld me to read it to me mother, and I said I would."

.   .   .   .   .   .

I had gone into the next room to see a poor woman who was lying very ill, and as neither Tim nor his mother spoke in a very low voice, I overheard the greater part of their conversation.

It was very gratifying to be an unseen witness to the fact that the effort of one of the Good Shepherd's dear lambs was having its effect, in inducing a conversation which could not fail to lead to some good result. Tim read to his mother the leaflet that had been given him. It was as follows :—

"THE WAY TO HEAVEN.

" Which is the way to heaven ?
  Dear mother, tell ;
Where children, all forgiven,
  In glory dwell.
Tell me, that I may run therein,
That I a glorious crown may win ;
  Tell me, dear mother, tell.

" Is that the glorious way ?
  Kind mother, tell ;
Marked on that solemn day
  The chariot fell.
Oh, tell me, and let me fly away
As Elijah, in chariot bright as day ;
  Mother, kind mother, tell.

" Or is that the gloomy road,
  Dear mother, tell,
Which the glorious martyrs trode,
  Defying hell ?
Tell me, and e'en the hottest flame
Shall prove my love for Jesus' name :
  Tell me, dear mother, tell."

" ANSWER.

" 'Tis not as Elijah rode,
  In chariot bright ;
Although he has reached the abode
  Of pure delight.
Nor are we called to tread the road,
Bearing the stains of martyr's blood,
  To heaven, so pure, so bright.

> " Believe, believe, dear child,
>   In God's dear Son ;
>   Hark ! Jesus, meek and mild,
>   Bids children come.
>   You'll find in Him the blessed way
>   That leads to everlasting day—
>   To heaven, to heaven, our home."

Thank God, said I to myself, that there are mothers who teach their children the way to heaven, and that there are ministers who do not forget to pray for the afflicted and the bereaved. Yes, and thank God that there are children who remember and repeat the lessons that they have been taught.

.   .   .   .   .   .

"I wish," said Mrs. O'Leary, "that I knew the way to hiven."

"Why, you *do* know it, mother. You towld me how to get there."

"Yes, I know I did; but it's all wrong—the ginnelman says it is."

"And he towld me so too, mother; only I didn't like to say so afore. He says there isn't any pruggerty."

" What does he say there is then ?"

"Why, he says that people go to hiven when they die."

"What! straight to hiven!"

"Yes, mother."

"But hiven's a long way off; don't he think there's a place to stop at afore we get there?"

"I don't know, mother. He says we can only get there through Jesus, and we can't get there any other way."

"Well, I don't know, I'm sure; I never heard the like iv it. It puts me all to sea. I have prayed every day for yer poor father, and I asks the blessed Virgin to make him a betther man. If it's no good o' going to Mary, I don't know what to do. It makes me feel wretched."

"Never mind, mother," said Tim, endeavouring to comfort her; "let's ask Jesus right straight. I wish the ginnelman would come agin and talk to us."

"So he will, Tim; he says he will."

"I'm glad o' that; I wish he'd give me father a talking to."

"It's no use iv anybody talking to yer father,

Tim. I'm tired o' that. Nobody can't do him any good."

"But the ginnelman talks so nicely, mother; me father couldn't help minding him."

"Perhaps he'd listen; but then it bothers me, because he says it's no good iv praying to Mary, and we must get some one to pray to for him."

"Perhaps, mother, some little girl like her I've seen to-day 'll pray for him night and morning; and the praste 'll pray for him."

"But the praste prays to Mary, ye know, and that won't do."

"Mary is deaf, mother, isn't she?" said Tim, inquiringly.

"Hush, Tim; mind what ye say. The blessed Virgin may curse us."

"I ain't afeerd, mother. It's sartin sure she don't mind what we say, or else she would ask her Son to make me father betther. I know I ask her properly."

"And so do I; and I'd give the world if I could only get Mary to persuade Jesus to make poor father sober and kind. But it don't seem iv any use, and I get tired iv asking."

"She don't hear us, mother; or else we're too poor for her to notice."

Mrs. O'Leary sighed. "Och, Tim," said she, "what'll we do?"

"Let's ask the little girl to pray for us—she prays for everybody, and she said her parson prayed for everybody, too; and he don't ask Mary—he asks Jesus straight; and perhaps he'll ask Jesus to make me poor father a betther man."

"May be he will," said she, slowly and in almost a whisper. "Hark! there's yer father on the stairs." And both listened.

"Don't he come up steady, mother?" said Tim; "perhaps it ain't him afther all."

It was, however; and he had reached the door almost before they were aware of it. Yes—and, to their great surprise, he was sufficiently sober to put a sentence together so as to be understood.

"Oh, father," said Tim, as the poor man entered the room, "what a thrate to have ye come home so soon!"

"A fine thrate. I'd be thinking ye had sooner see the back of me any day."

" Not that at all, at all," said his wife, cheerfully.   " We were just talking about ye, and
wishing ye stayed at home more."

" Yes, father," said Tim ; " and we are going to
get somebody to ask God to bless ye. A ginnelman we've seen will be sure to pray for you if
we ask him."

" A ginnelman pray for me ! I never heard
the like of it. Oh, no, no—no ginnelman 'll
pray for me. A man may find something betther to trouble himself about than praying for
me. I ain't worth it, nohow. Besides, what's
the good iv asking Mary ? she can't do anything."

" Well," said Mrs. O'Leary, " that's sthrange :
we have just been thinking ourselves what's the
good iv asking Mary, she don't hear us ; or if she
does, she does not care about them that's poor
and ain't got any money to pay well for a good
answer."

" All right," said Mr. O'Leary ; " ye're not such
fools afther all as I thought ye were."

" See what the ginnelman has done," said Tim ;
" he's given me some money to buy a loaf, and I

had a penny change out, and so I bought some cheese."

"Yes, father," said Mrs. O'Leary, "for once let us sit down and have a meal together."

They all sat on the floor; and, drunkard as he was, the father showed that, after all, he had a heart, for the tears ran down his cheeks.

Scanty as was the meal, it was evidently eaten with a relish, but in silence.

.   .   .   .   .

The next day was the sabbath.

CHAPTER IV.

O'LEARY'S VISIT TO A SUNDAY SCHOOL, AND WHAT CAME OF IT.

MR. O'LEARY was out by nine o'clock. Tim and his mother trembled when they heard him say he should take a walk so early as nine o'clock on Sunday morning; but Mrs. O'Leary thought it best not to say anything to her husband, hoping that he might remember what they had talked about on the previous evening. She knew, moreover, that no public-house would be open for some hours, and could not help sighing the wish that they were not open at all, on Sundays at least.

Tim went to the ragged school that day for the first time. He was very kindly received, and enjoyed the day very much, saying that he never felt so happy on a Sunday before.

The father wandered about until nearly eleven o'clock, evidently much agitated in mind. At

C

THE SUNDAY SCHOOL.

length, seeing the door of a schoolroom open, he entered. The teacher was at the desk, and the children were singing a hymn The poor man sat down, and seemed deeply interested, and once or twice was heard to say to himself, but sufficiently loud to be heard, "Beautiful, beautiful I I wish Tim was here, that I do!"

He sat till the children began to sing the closing hymn, when he rose and hurried out. Much to the surprise of all, however, when the school had reassembled for the afternoon teaching, and had stood up to sing the first hymn, the same individual entered and took his seat near the door. He watched the countenances of the children very narrowly, as if endeavouring to trace the effect of the engagement on their minds. At length his eye rested upon two bright-eyed girls who appeared to unite in the singing with all their souls. The words were,—

> "My parents, Lord, are kind to me,
>   They tell me of Thy love ;
> Oh, may they both be dear to Thee,
>   And all Thy goodness prove."

"Dear to Thee," said O'Leary. "Dear to God,

niver : that O'Leary 'll niver be able to say ;"
and he buried his head in his hands.

At the conclusion of the opening service the
superintendent went up to him, and in mild and
gentle tones inquired, "What makes you weep,
my friend ?"

" I can never be dear to Him."

"What do you mean, friend ?"

"I am a drunkard—a wretch—without a penny.
I am a drunkard.   Dear to Him—no, niver !   My
wife clings to me, and so does my poor boy.   But,
as we used to say down our country, it shticks
like a burr to us.   I've pawned everything till we
ain't got nothing, not a chair nor a table.   Me
boy, it's he as strives hard to keep a roof over
his poor mother's head.   Oh, I wish he was here,
sir ; it 'd do him good."   And the poor man
sobbed aloud.

"Oh, sir," continued he, "will ye pray for me
—a wretch like me ?"

"I will," said the superintendent ; but as any
further conversation would have interfered with
school engagements, he promised to speak with
the man afterwards.

"I'll go home, then, sir," said he, "and tell 'em ye're coming."

Mr. F. did not intend to go to the poor man's house that day, but as it was evident the poor fellow had made up his mind to it, he said he would be there shortly.

"But you must tell me where I am to come to," said Mr. F.; and the man directed him to the very house where Tim had led him on a former occasion.

"Then you are the father of Tim, the boy that sells papers," said the superintendent. "I will come with greater pleasure now, if possible."

Full of gratitude, he thought, Here is an answer to the poor boy's prayer. God will hear prayer. O Lord, make my visit of much service to this man.

At half-past five he wended his way to the wooden house in the dark alley.

Scarcely had I entered the room — for you must know that I was the superintendent referred to—than the poor man grasped my hand, and said in a low, fervent tone, "I wanted to spake to ye, sir: God bless ye for iver."

"Well," said I, "to tell you the truth, I have felt deeply interested in you ever since your son pointed you out to me, as you stood listening to a lecturer addressing the people on temperance in the streets."

"God bless ye, sir," said he, "and it's me guardian angel that he is—he's saved me ; he doesn't know how, but he has ;" and he fairly broke down as he spoke, the tears running freely over his rough cheeks.

"Blessed be God for the child.   It's the patient, kind boy he's been since he was that high, and shame to me that I ain't treated him like a human being !   But oh, sir, ye don't know what an angel he's been ;—again he had a struggle with his emotions, while for the moment I was too much affected to speak.   Presently the man continued,—" Many's the time he's fetched me home o' nights when I've been that bad that I should ha' been froze afore mornin' ;   and many's the time he's brought me somethin' to ate when I ha' been lying on that straw in the corner there, cursing and swearing away as if there wasn't ather God or devil.   And he's that patient, sir,—that patient, that if I'd kicked him from one end o' the room to the other, he'd never turn upon me, nor say a bad word. He's been me guardian angel every minnit of my drunken life."

During all this time the boy stood with his hands in his pockets, looking down on the floor, and apparently uncomfortable. For however much he deserved to be thus spoken of, he seemed to feel that he had only done his duty.

The father noticed this likewise. "I want to spake to ye, sir," said he; and begged of me to be so good as to let him say a word to me alone.

"Very pleased shall I be to do so," was my reply; "but where can we go?"

This was soon arranged; for his wife and boy went away a few moments to "sit with a neighbour."

"God bless ye for iver," said the poor man, in fervent tones; and again drawing a hard breath, repeated, "God bless ye for iver, sir. It was my angel of a boy that stopped me. What do ye think, sir? Why, one morning, after I had been batin' him, I found a bit o' paper pinned to my rag of a coat ; it was this as I holds in my hand, sir. Tim had picked it up somewhere, I don't know where. However, that's no matter. I took and read it as well as I could. Here it is, sir ; read it, plase."

I took it, and read as follows :—

> " Dear father, drink no more, I pray,
>   It makes you look so sad ;
>   Come home, and drink no more, I say,
>   'Twill make poor mother glad.
>
> " Dear father, think how ill you've been,
>   What aches and pains you've had !
>   Oh, ' drink no more,' unless you mean
>   To drive dear mother mad.
>
> " Dear father, think me not unkind
>   When I entreat you so ;
>   Oh, 'drink no more,' and then you'll find
>   A home where'er you go.
>
> " Dear father, think of mother's tears,
>   How oft and sad they flow !
>   Oh, ' drink no more,' then will her fears
>   No longer rack her so.
>
> " Dear father, think what would become
>   Of me, were you to die ;
>   Without a father, or a home,
>   Or friend beneath the sky !

" Dear father, do not turn away,
   Nor from me think to roam;
  Oh, ' drink no more' by night or day;
   Now come, let us go home.

" Dear father, ' drink no more,' I pray,
   It makes you look so sad;
  Come home, and ' drink no more,' I say,
   'Twill make that home so glad.

" Thus spoke in tenderness the child—
   The drunkard's heart was moved;
  He signed the pledge, he wept, he smiled,
   And kissed the boy he loved."

" Well, sir," said he, as I returned the paper to him, "that bit made me wretched. If Tim had run a knife into me, I think I could have stood it better; yes, I do, and without flinching too. Do you think a child ever preached a better sarmint to his father without saying anything?"

" It was certainly a very quiet way of reading you a lesson, showing you how he felt and what he wished."

" Ay, it was; and it's I that 'll niver forgit it; no, niver as long as I live. I hardly knows now how to look him or his poor mother in the face, sich a wretch I've been to them."

" But," said I, "no doubt they forgive you;

and you must prove that you are really sorry
for the unkind, cruel conduct shown them,
by doing so no more. You must give up the
habit which has brought such misery on you and
yours, and let the last two lines of the hymn be
true in respect to you,—

> ' He signed the pledge, he wept, he smiled,
>   And kissed the boy he loved.' "

"That I'll do; the little angel. I won't take
another drop, niver another, that I won't. But
then, sir, I know that 'll niver mend the mischief
I've done. D'ye think, sir, I can be forgiven?
Don't ye think I shall be clear shut out of
hiven?"

"I hope not," was my reply to the latter question. "Jesus says, 'Him that cometh to Me I
will in no wise cast out.'"

"That may be true enough about thim as
comes; but then *I* haven't come, ye see. Besides, I heard a man say that it was written in
the Book that drunkards 'll not go to hiven;
and I've been a drunkard these ten years."

"Yet, notwithstanding, you may be saved, and
go to heaven."

"Wisha, how'll that be, sir?" said the poor man. "If the Bible's thrue, the door 'll be slammed in me face as soon as I gets near it, if I am bould enough to go to ask to be let in. But I don't suppose I'll ever have the chance o' getting near enough even for that."

I assured him that the Bible holds out hope for the worst of men. But he persisted that there was no hope for such as he.

"If you repent, and turn away from your evil course," I observed, "if you leave off sinning, God will receive you, and be very gracious to you. I know the Bible says that drunkards will not be admitted to heaven. That does not mean that the man who ceases to be a drunkard before he dies will not—oh no. It means that none who die in their sins, drunkards, swearers, or liars, can enter heaven."

The poor fellow stood silent for a while; then, at length, as if beginning to comprehend the meaning of the passage, said, "Is this the way, sir? In the afternoon I heerd you say, as the tree falls down, so it 'll lie; and you said, if a man died a very bad man, he couldn't then be made a good man; and I've been thinking that you'd say that if a man dies a good man, he couldn't be made a bad man after death."

"Quite right; and whatever sins may have stained your character, if you do not die in your sins you will be saved."

"Then I'll sign the pledge," said he, and he evidently meant what he said.

"The safest thing you can do," said I, "the *only* safe thing for such as you."

"Well, sir, I hope it is; I don't want to die a drunkard, anyhow."

"But," I added, "desirable as it is that you should sign the pledge, and much as it will be to your advantage to do so, you must remember that will not save your soul, nor obtain for you the favour of God."

"Then, if I give up drinking, sha'n't I go to hiven when I die?"

"I hope you will," said I; "but it would not be *because* you gave up drinking."

Saying thus much, I told him that I should leave him for the present. However, he begged me to step in and bid his wife and boy good

night, and to pray with them before I left.
This I cheerfully consented to, and commended
them all to the care of Him who is able to save
to the uttermost them that come unto God by
Him.

As I was returning to my own abode these
lines came into my mind,—

> " Petitions are good as far as they go,
>   But they feed not the hungry poor;
> Good wishes are good as far as they go,
>   But a blessing to bless must be more:
> A blessing to bless both giver and gift
>   Must be shared from our own little store."

And acting upon this suggestion of the poet, as
soon as I reached my home I asked that what
remained of broken victuals might be shown me.
There proved to be sufficient for a meal for the
poor repentant drunkard, and such a one as his
wife and child might enjoy with him.

I sent it, therefore, immediately to the house
I had just left.

CHAPTER V.

"Tim," said Mr. O'Leary the next morning, "just run up to the ginnelman as lectures, and ask him whether it 'll be convanient for him to see me sign the pledge."

Tim stood amazed ; but, nevertheless, did not require to have the message repeated. He was off in a twinkling ; nor was he many moments gone.

"Come now," said he, almost out of breath, "come *now*, father ; the ginnelman says you are to come *now*."

"And what else ? "

"Why, he said, because it's always best to strike while the iron is hot. But that's a funny thing to say ; what does he mean ? "

"Well, Tim, I think I can tell ye. When I

was a boy I went to church; and one day I heerd the parson—our parson was as good a Christian as ever lived,—I heerd him say that when iron is red-hot you can bend it to your mind, but when it gets cold you can't bend it nohow."

"That's just it," said Mrs. O'Leary, who sat hoping and fearing—hoping that her husband would perform his resolution, fearing lest when he reached the street he should alter his mind. "That's just it: it's best to do a thing when ye're in the mind for it, bekase if ye puts it off ye mayn't do it at all."

"Come along, father," said Tim; "I'll go with you."

"So ye shall, me guardian angel;" and brushing the tears from his eyes, he hurried down the street, Tim leading the way, to the lecturer's house.

"So you wish to give up a bad habit, and sign the pledge," said the good man.

"If you plase, sir, and it's convanient to you."

"Quite convenient, my good man. Why, I

can tell you that I have more than once turned
out of my bed at night to help to reclaim
a drunkard."

"My father's not a drunkard now," said Tim,
a little indignant.

"I did not mean that he was; but your
father will understand me.   I want to show him
how pleased I am, and that it *is* quite convenient
to me to do as he wishes."

With that he went to his desk, and taking
therefrom a printed form, placed it before his
visitor.   Tim read as follows :—

I,   , promise and vow
never more to taste any intoxicating drink.   This I do in the
presence of
   Date   Signed,
   Witnessed by

With a trembling hand he filled up the blank
space after the letter I, and signed his name at
the foot of the paper.   There was determination
mingled with fear in the act.   He seemed fully
aware of the solemnity of the deed; and when
his only child signed his name as a witness, he
fairly sobbed aloud.

TIM REALIZES HIS POSITION. 57

"God help you to keep your pledge," said the lecturer. "I trust He will, sir," said O'Leary.

"He will if you ask Him. Mind, keep out of bad company. Don't get inside the alehouse; if ye go there, it's all a chance if ye'll be able to keep the ale out of you."

"I'll try to do so, sir. I'll keep as far away as iver I can."

.   .   .   .   .

"Oh," said O'Leary, as he sat down on his returning home, realizing more than ever his position, "a pretty kittle of fish we are in. Nothing to eat. Nothing to do. All me own doing. Oh, Tim, ye've got a bad father."

"A betther father now than he had a week ago," said Mrs. O'Leary—"a *real* father."

"But nothing to do. My drinking ways have lost me all me work, and no one 'll employ me; they'll be afeerd to."

"Don't say that, father," said Tim; "you'll get something to do. Why, the ginnelman who came to see us 'll do something for us."

"May be; but then I don't want to be too imposing on his good nature."

"The ginnelman has been and gone," said Mrs. O'Leary, "and what do ye think? He says, if ye'll go up to his house afore ten to-morrow morning, he's found a place for you, a sort o' portering place."

"There, father," exclaimed Tim, "didn't I say so?"

O'Leary was at first too much overcome to speak; at length he broke out,—

"I don't desarve it! don't desarve it!—not I —don't desarve it. It's all for your sake, Tim, and yer mother's. Ye desarve it; and I'll work me flesh off me bones if that 'll keep ye from starving, that I will, if I can only get the work to do. Ye sha'n't starve—ye sha'n't starve, if hard work 'll buy a crust for ye."

His wife was amazed to hear such passionate exclamations from one who but a short time before had abused her in terms equally strong, and had used that strength which he was now so ready to spend in obtaining for her the necessaries of life in ill-using and driving her from her own home.

But it was even so. Bitterly did O'Leary

repent himself; and his repentance was sincere, inasmuch as he forsook the habit he had so long cherished ; and that notwithstanding much petty persecution and annoyance.

As many more have done, O'Leary found that a new situation, although it introduces to new companions, introduces to new temptations.

" Well, O'Leary," said Jim Howard, "of course you'll pay your footing."

"Not I," was the rejoinder, "I have paid away in drink already till I've got no footing anywhere."

" But it's the rule," said Jim.

"And it's a rule that I don't intend to mind, then," said O'Leary.

"But you must pay down the money, even if you don't choose to give drink," observed Will Kelly ; " that's only fair."

"I don't intend to do that nather," replied O'Leary.

"Oh, let the stingy fellow alone," said Dick Turnaway ; "let him keep his money to hisself, and much good may it do him."

O'Leary did not like to be thought mean ; hence

he was half inclined to pay the money as soon as he got any, in order to get rid of his tempters. But a moment's thought showed him that such a course would never do. He must manfully and at once resist this new temptation, at all costs. He therefore positively refused to " pay his footing."

In consequence of this decision he had to endure many a gibe and many a sneer. Ay, for weeks, and even months, scarcely a day passed but there was the temptation to join with his fellow-workmen in some "drinking" bout or other ; but happily in vain was it presented to O'Leary.

A day came, however, which sorely tried him. His employer gave his men a day ; indeed, they went down to a country inn, where a sumptuous dinner was provided, and at which one of the firm presided. Of course O'Leary was there.

Now it happened that the president was not an abstainer, but had been exceedingly kind to O'Leary.

" Let us drink," said he, as they sat at dinner, "to the health of O'Leary. He is a new hand, but a very diligent one ; and therefore I hope you will all join heartily with me in drinking to the health of O'Leary."

All eyes were turned upon him, and glasses were not only sipped, but emptied. We shall not stop to inquire into the feelings which probably actuated some who drank to O'Leary's health—they may be readily conceived. Our readers will be prepared to believe that some were already beginning to chuckle over the poor man, and felt sure of his fall, since he could never refuse "the governor."

O'Leary — to his honour be it stated — did refuse the governor. Being called upon to reply to the toast, he asked if he might be allowed a little water. His request was granted, although somewhat reluctantly. O'Leary then addressed his employer and fellow-workmen after the following manner :—

"Sir, I can't drink no beer nor nothing o' the sort. I have drunk too much o' that already. I've spoilt me home, and half starved me wife and boy, and they'd ha' been starved the other half if it had not been for that guardian angel iv a boy that took to selling papers; and it's all

through him that I'm not rolling about the
streets now, instead o' standing here, and being
with you every day earning an honest penny.

"I'm intirely obliged to you, sir, and to my
companions here for your good wishes, and I
hope you won't think any the worse o' me
because I only drink wather; and if ye'll allow
me I'll drink to all your good healths. I'll do
my best to give the governor as good, or even a
betther day's work than any of you, although ye
drink beer. Here's to the health of the governor
and all of you."

All eyes were turned on the "governor," and
some felt sure that O'Leary would get a good
roasting now. But they were disappointed.

"O'Leary," said Mr. Jackson, "I thank you,
and you his workfellows, for the manner in which
my health has been proposed and in which the
toast has been received. It is a good thing when
a master enjoys the confidence of his workmen.
It is not always easy, on such occasions as the
present, to distinguish between what may be
mere form and flattery and what is genuine. To-
day, however, I am inclined to believe that one

at least is no flatterer. I refer to O'Leary. He has abided by his own principles; and although he stands alone, he has manfully avowed that he will not, whatever we may do, touch intoxicating drinks to please anybody. I thought well of O'Leary before, but I think better of him now. I shall have confidence in him as a sober, honest servant, and I trust he will be spared to prove that my confidence has not been misplaced.

"Let me entreat you all—Resolve as O'Leary has done; and if you make up your minds to try and do your work as he does upon water, I shall be rather pleased than otherwise. For my own part, I'm inclined to give much consideration to the subject."

. . . . . .

"Betther than all my fears," said O'Leary, on reaching home that evening. "I niver felt so bad in my life as I did when the governor told 'em to drink me health; for I was sure they'd expect me to drink, and nothing would please Kelly and them better than to see me in a fix. Howsomdever, I didn't think I could ha' spoken as I did. I was helped, I don't know how."

"It wasn't Mary helped you, was it, father?" said Tim.

"No, boy, I never asked her; but I'm sartin sure, if somebody hadn't, I could never have stood it, but should have been persuaded into drinking again."

"Father," said Tim, "I saw Patrick O'Brien to-day, and he said, 'What's the odds if you do get drunk? Mary 'll allays forgive ye. It's only to pay the praste a trifle, and it 'll be all right. Why shouldn't ye enjoy yerself?' But I tould him it's no good o' going to Mary, she don't hear us."

"Yes, ye're right, Tim; it's a pack o' nonsense to ask Mary, I'm sartin sure o' that."

"And the ginnelman said no one but Jesus could do anything to help us. It's o' no use asking any one but Him."

.   .   .   .   .   .

In the morning O'Leary went to his work as usual; but how different a reception did he meet with now from that which greeted him formerly! His companions were more respectful; and from that day forward there was a marked improvement in the habits of all his workfellows.

D

O'LEARY'S HOME.

CHAPTER VI.

MRS. O'LEARY gradually gathered together many little home comforts, and rejoiced in the opportunity she now possessed of proving to her husband how thrifty a wife was his. It became her habitual study to make everything go as far as possible. She was not mean nor niggardly, but by the exercise of a wise economy she succeeded in providing many a nourishing and even savoury meal, and withal to give some little help to the needy.

O'Leary's appearance soon became so respectable as to lead not a few to suppose that he was receiving a larger income than many of his fellow-workmen. Indeed, Kelly began to be jealous of him, and to annoy him in various ways.

" What are you the better for drinking water ?"

said he one day as they stood working side by
side.   " I suppose you think yourself wiser than
we are."

Kelly had suffered an envious spirit to obtain
the mastery, and to lead him to say what, in
calmer moments, he would confess to be very
wide of the truth. O'Leary, however, very meekly
replied,—

" Well, to be candid, Kelly, I have *lost* a great
deal by it. I have lost my slouched hat, and
ragged coat, and shoes with scarcely a bit of sole
to 'em ; and I've lost the habit o' drinkin'. I
used to try to get up a quarrel with everybody I
met, and that habit *you* know I've lost."

" Yes, to be sure," said Kelly, "and it is just
that that makes you think yourself wiser than us."

" No, Kelly, I am not wiser than you ; I never
knew you to get drunk at all : and so you are a
long way ahead iv me. It was wiser of you
not to get drunk than it was for me to leave off
the habit o' drinkin'."

" Well, to be sure, I never did, thank God,"
said Kelly, softening his manner ; "perhaps you
are right."

"And then," continued O'Leary, "my wife has lost a great deal."

"Your wife, O'Leary; a lot *she* had to lose! Why, poor thing, you kept her out of every far-thing, and she hadn't enough to put on to make her decent; and if it hadn't been for young Tim, you'd ha' lost *her* long ago."

"I know that; I'm sartin sure o' that, Kelly; but still she has lost an aching heart, for that she often had afore I signed the pledge."

"Well, I think you are right there; for she seems allays a deal happier now, as far as I can judge, than ever she was in her life."

"She *is*, Kelly, and so am I; and my home is a deal more comfortable."

"So it ought to be," said Kelly; "for you are a favourite with the governor, and get better wages than we do."

"I don't think I do," O'Leary replied; "it hasn't anything to do with the wages. It's my wife's way iv doing things, and that you'll be able to prove some day!"

Kelly soon had an opportunity of satisfying himself that he had judged his workfellow wrongfully. O'Leary having sprained his ankle, Kelly was entrusted to convey to O'Leary his wages week by week; for Mr. Jackson was very considerate, and while encouraging his men to "provide against a rainy day," did not forsake them in their hour of distress, but continued their wages, when satisfied that they were really incapable of work.

Said Kelly one day, as he sat in O'Leary's room, "I can't think how it is you manages so well. You haven't so much a week as I have, and yet you have more about you than I have got."

"Well, Kelly, it's by givin' me wife all the money to do it with. Since I have given up drinkin', I haven't needed much for meself, so I hand over all except a shilling or two."

"And do ye mane to say that you owe it all to your wife's management?"

"I do, Kelly; and yours is just such a wife as mine is, if ye'd only trust her."

"No, no, Kelly; that can't be it nohow."

"But I believe she is," said O'Leary; "thry her, and see if I am not right in the main."

The fact was, Kelly thought he could manage best himself, and hence bought this thing and the other, without regard as to whether it was wanted or not, or whether he had value for his money. On the other hand, his wife was a meek creature, and would do or suffer anything rather than find fault. Hence things went on in a very unsatisfactory manner, and their life was one continual struggle, when all might have been comfortable. Both husband and wife were wrong—not for not finding fault, but for not setting about to discover how it was that they could not make both ends meet.

"I'll try," said Kelly, "to do as you say. I'll let Jinnie have all I can spare, and see what she'll do with it."

He was as good as his word. Nor did he repent it. His wife, encouraged by the confidence placed in her, set to work in good earnest to make the best of her husband's earnings. The result was, that they became total abstainers, although they did not sign the pledge.

There was, however, one fault in both families. Deriving so much enjoyment and comfort in consequence of their change of habits, they began to build their hopes of eternal happiness upon their temperate and moral course of life. The priest, who had called more than once, finding that he could not convince them that it was of any use to pray to the Virgin, did his best to foster these feelings of self-righteousness by telling Mrs. O'Leary that there might be a reason why Mary would not hear them, and perhaps it was that they had not done enough to merit her good offices. He was glad, however, at last to discover that they were in the right way, and he could assure them that before long they would know that Mary did hear them, by the help they received in various ways.

Mrs. O'Leary told this to her husband. He, however, was keen enough to see through the priest's sophistry.

"Wife," said he, "don't talk with that man; don't believe him. Depind on't we're wrong; I'm sure we are, or else he wouldn't say we're right."

"D'ye think so?" said she.

"I do; and when the ginnelman comes— and I've asked him to—as was in the Sunday school and helped us, you'll see what he says about it."

"When d'ye expect him? I'll be afther doin' me best for him."

"He's comin' on Saturday afternoon; you know that is our leisure afternoon now."

. . . . .

It was a happy meeting when Mr. F. entered the dwelling of Mr. and Mrs. O'Leary, and not a little honoured did they feel in being allowed to show hospitality to one to whom they were so greatly indebted. In the course of conversation, O'Leary broached the question as to the good they got by being temperate.

Mr. F. soon perceived that both were viewing a life of temperance too much as a life of godliness. "Remember," said he, gravely, "temperance is not Christianity—temperance will not save you, although it may help you in the way."

"Well," said O'Leary, "I was beginning to think we were going wrong, and in fact I made up my mind to ask you a little about it, bekase the praste said we should find Mary did hear us,

bekase we were doing all we could to save ourselves."

"Good works won't secure God's favour. You
may live a sober life, and die sober, but you
cannot be saved in any other way than through
Christ. Mary can't hear you ; and certain I am
God won't, unless you have repented of your sins,
and come to Him depending entirely and alone
on what Christ has done for you.

"Don't you see the difference? The priest says
Mary don't hear you because you haven't done
enough. The Bible says, ' By grace ye are saved,
through faith ; not of works, lest any man should
boast.' All that God requires of you and me
is that we should come to Him just as we are,
confessing and forsaking our sins, and trusting
in what Jesus has done for us, and we shall
find mercy. All the good deeds in the world
will not save you, O'Leary. 'There is none other
name given among men whereby we must be
saved.' There is no mediator but Jesus. It won't
do to have anything between your soul and Jesus."

"You see," said O'Leary, "Mary expects so
much of us ; and then, as you say, she can't help

us ; and it comes to this, that if we depind on what we does ourselves, we are as much as sayin' we can save ourselves. I see,—I see, sir. It won't do to think that bekase we are temperance people God 'll save us."

"Right, O'Leary. It would be a much harder way, were it a way at all, to be saved through Mary, than it is to be saved through Jesus. As you said just now, Mary expects so much of you. Jesus says, 'He that believeth shall be saved.'"

O'Leary and his wife at length learned the way of the Lord more perfectly, and there is no doubt that they are now both followers of the meek and lowly Jesus. Our readers, however, may like to know what became of Tim O'Leary. We may tell them in a few words.

We have already stated that Tim went to the ragged school, and it was on the first Sunday that his father had been sober for six years. The teacher's subject that day was Jesus' invitation to children, and the lesson was founded on Mark x. 13—16. Among other questions the teacher asked,—

"Why should children come to Christ ?"

"For the same reason as grown-up people should," said a sharp lad.

"Well, my boy," said Mr. Jones, turning to Tim, "and what do *you* think?"

"Me mother says as the praste says, we've no right to ask Jesus for anything."

"Who then are we to ask?"

"The blessed Virgin."

"Oh no, my lad," said the teacher, earnestly but kindly; we must go to Jesus, old or young, whoever we are. We are all sinners, and need a Saviour. What did Jesus come into the world for?"

"To save souls, sir."

"Just so; and why do souls need saving?"

"Bekase of sin, sir."

"Children sin, do they not?"

"Yes, sir," said Tim, "but not as bad as their fathers do."

"You are mistaken there, my boy. Children as much need to go to Jesus to get their souls saved as men and women. They should ask His forgiveness for the sins they have done."

"No, sir," said Tim, "it ain't right to do that;

the praste says we must ask the blessed Virgin to
spake to Him for us. I've asked her agin and
agin, but she don't seem to hear me, or else me
father would have been a bether man long ago."

"It is right to pray for your parents, but to
be heard you must do so in God's way, and that
is through Jesus Christ. You can only be saved
through Him. Let me beg of you all to think
very seriously about this matter. Each of you
has a soul that will never die; it is lost by sin, but
Jesus Christ is willing to save it. In forty years,
perhaps, every one of us here will be gone from
this world; some of us, perhaps, very soon; nobody knows how soon; certainly in a few years,
another set of teachers, and another set of scholars,
will have come—but will your soul be dead
then?"

"No."

"Where should you like it to be?"

"With Jesus."

"That depinds," said Tim.

"Depends upon what?" asked his teacher.

"Why, if ye don't get clear o' pruggerty ye'll
be *there*."

"But we don't believe in purgatory," said the teacher. "The Bible tells us that when we die, we shall go either to heaven or hell. If we die without going to Jesus, we shall certainly not be allowed to go to Him then. We cannot go to Him now as the Jewish children we have been reading about did. But we can go to Him in thought; by thinking about Him, by praying to Him ; and He is watching our thoughts, and waiting to answer our prayers. It is only by going to Him in this world that we can hope to go to Him in the next."

All the time his teacher was speaking, Tim felt that he should like to go to Jesus ; and he did as was wished —went home, and thought a great deal about Jesus. He took much to reading his Bible : it became to him a very precious book. Often did he sing to the air, "We're a band of brothers," the verses closing thus,—

> " There's a book, of all books dearest,
>   To my bosom I press nearest,
>   '*Tis the Bible*, he who clearest
>   Understands its truths is blest.
>   What a thrilling story,

Of shame and glory,
Is opened before me,
In the book I love the best!"

Tim soon won his teacher's esteem, who obtained him a situation, where he first acted as errand boy, and in after years rose to the position of an overseer.

Many things in his character are deserving of our notice; a few of them I will mention. In modesty he was a pattern to all. His mind was of a thoughtful and meditative cast. There was a marked caution in his words and actions, and a marked tenderness in his feelings and sympathies. Dutiful and obedient as a son, he was anxious to comply with the wishes of his parents when with them; and when absent from them, would often speak of them in the most affectionate and endearing manner.

"As a friend he was warm-hearted, and friends he did not easily forget. At school he was diligent and manly, and was sorely grieved if he could not learn the lesson his teachers set him. In play he was never rough and unfair, but always gentle and upright, and thus he won the confidence and esteem of his playfellows, and became their favourite. It would seem as though he constantly kept this couplet before his mind,—

> ' Be open, generous, just, and true,
> In all you think, and say, and do.' "

It was a long time, however, before Tim learned that amiability is not piety, and that a person may be all you could wish him to be, short of truly pious ; and he was not a little distressed at times ; nor did he obtain true peace of mind until he had learned to believe, as well as do and pray.

Tim is now an earnest follower of the Saviour, trusting in the alone merits of his death for salvation.

London : J & W. Rider, Printers, 14, Bartholomew Close, E.C.

www.ingramcontent.com/pod-product-compliance
Lightning Source LLC
Chambersburg PA
CBHW020236090426
42735CB00010B/1711